Our App

by Carol Pugliano
illustrated by Carol Koeller

My family has an apple tree.
This is the story of how
it grew.

I helped Dad plant an apple seed.
Apple seeds are small.
But they grow to be big trees.

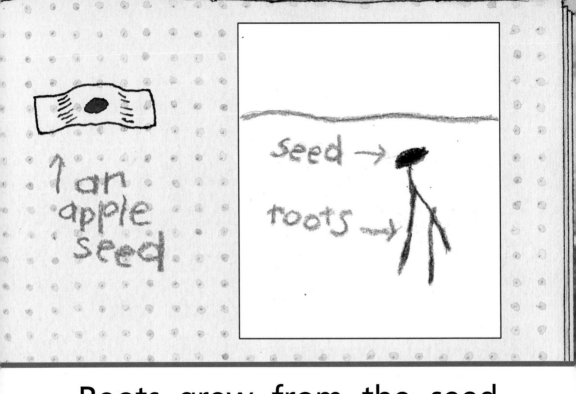

Roots grew from the seed. The roots grew down into the soil.

A small stem grew from
the seed.
Stems are like straws.
They bring water to the tree.

The stem grew into a
small tree.
It got bigger. I did, too.
I was as big as the tree!

One spring, flowers grew on the tree.

The flowers became
red apples.

When I grow up, I will
have my own family.
We will grow an apple
tree, too!